The Healing Power of Sleep!

A guide to healthy and refreshing sleep skills

Lynn D. Johnson, Ph.D.
Director, Brief Therapy Center of Utah

Published by
Head Acre Press
166 East 5900 South
Suite B-108
Salt Lake City, UT 84107 U.S.A.
(801) 261-1412

Library of Congress Cataloging-in-Publication Data
Johnson, Lynn D.
The Healing Power of Sleep:
A guide to healthy and refreshing sleep skills
ISBN 978-0-9762734-2-4
1. Sleep hygiene. 2. Self-help. 3. Title

Printed in the United States of America
1 2 3 4 5 6 7 8 9 10

ISBN 13: 978-0-9762734-2-4
ISBN 10: 9762734-2-4

Head Acre Press books are available at special quantity discounts to use as premiums and promotions or for use in training programs. Please write to Director of Sales, Head Acre Press, 166 East 5900 South, B-108, SLC, UT 84107

Additional information about this book is on the website, www.SleepingSkills.com

Advance Praise for *The Healing Power of Sleep*

"Whether you have trouble sleeping yourself or know somebody who does, Lynn Johnson's book, *The Healing Power of Sleep* is a fantastic resource. It is a very accessible book, packed with practical tools that you can use right away to help you get the sleep you need. This is the first resource I would turn to for sleep troubles of any kind. I can't recommend this book highly enough."

> – Joel F. Wade, Ph.D. Author of "Mastering Happiness: Ten Principles for Living a More Fulfilling Life."

"So many times when asked to comment on a book I've wanted to say, "This book is a real yawner." Finally, I can do so without being rude to a colleague. Not only is the book filled with excellent advice, it is also engaging; Dr. Johnson talks directly to his readers. His 12 rules for good sleep distill lots of solid research, clinical experience, and old-fashioned common sense into practical guidelines. From diet to exercise to meditation, he urges readers to do what works, and to keep track of what works! If you have trouble sleeping, you would do well to read this book and follow the good advice you will find."

> – Todd Essig, Ph.D., Training and Supervising Analyst, William Alanson White Institute

"If you're up at 3 a.m. or treating someone who is then this book must be on your night stand! Dr. Johnson does a fabulous job putting together everything useful you need to know about relieving your insomnia. I've already had clients get a good night's sleep after just two days of using the Autogenic Training."

> – Elizabeth Gessel, MFT

"Dr Lynn Johnson's latest book put me to sleep. And, why shouldn't it? *The Healing Power of Sleep* is an excellent self help book on the treatment of insomnia. In an engaging, easy to read and motivational style, Dr Johnson offers precise, step by step guidance on how to address and overcome insomnia. His book is comprehensive. Among the many topics covered are the importance of sleep, how bad habits contribute to the problem and how we can change them. It also includes up-to- date research about diet, exercise and meditation as well as addressing the problem of snoring. (His 'how to meditate' chapter is an additional bonus!) This book provides constant encouragement to practice newly learned skills. All in all, who would have thought a book about sleep would be such a page turner! I highly recommend this book to anyone who wants a good night's sleep without pharmaceuticals."
– Ellen Rabinowich LCSW

"Our sleep-deprived, blackberry, tweeting, facebook generation desperately needs this book. Sleep deprivation has serious side effects: it impairs our immune system, and interferes with our being able to handle stress as well as our emotions. Dr. Johnson helps readers develop effective sleep habits in very practical ways so that they can keep pace with the demands of career, family and the ever-changing pressures of technology. A must read for anyone who is perpetually tired!"
– Barbara McFarland, Ed.D.

"This is a wonderful book on sleep, one I will strongly recommend to clients. It will certainly help."
– Lonny Stanford, M.S.

Contents

Chapter One

The Magic of Sleep

Have you heard about the new wonder diet? Effortless weight loss! No need to change your eating habits. No need to exercise. You just sit on your couch and watch TV, and the excess pounds melt away! Does it sound too good to be true? It is! Of course, anything worth doing is going to take some effort. If you think that reading a short book on insomnia will cure you of sleep problems, you are in for a sad disappointment.

On the other hand, if you are willing to work at good sleep skills, collect some data, be a detective and figure out what is behind really good sleep, then your sleep will improve.

WHY THIS IS IMPORTANT

There are several reasons for you to take sleep seriously. Let's quickly review a few of them. And, you may ask, why do this? You would not be reading this if you didn't have concerns about your own sleep. Changing your sleep habits will require motivation on your part. Forming new habits isn't easy. One way to increase your motivation is to review reasons why change is valuable.

People who sleep well learn skills better. Dreaming is when you symbolically practice new skills. If you are learning, for example, to dance the tango, you will actually be better at the new steps the next morning.

People with good sleep habits are healthier and live

longer. One study found that patients who slept an average of only five hours a night had five times the risk of high blood pressure, compared with patients who slept more than six hours a night.

People who sleep poorly may develop circulation problems and calcium buildup in the arteries. In a University of Chicago Medical Center study, 12% of a group of people age 35-47 developed calcium buildup over five years. In those people sleeping five hours a night or less, 27% suffered buildup. But among people sleeping seven hours or more a night, only 6% showed calcium clogging their arteries.

People who get at least seven hours of sleep a night are more likely to resist infections, colds and flu. Adequate sleep encourages a healthier immune system.

Sleep problems are also a cause of obesity. People who miss sleep will eat more to make up for the lack of energy they experience. They prefer to eat foods high in sugar or fat, foods that might give them a burst of energy.

When you eat more, you really ought to work longer and harder. A candy bar of 250 calories will require walking at least three miles to "burn it off." If you are missing sleep, do you feel like walking that three miles to burn off the candy bar? Of course not. You want to lie around, probably eating more high-calorie food. So when you are short on sleep, you both eat too much and exercise less, a double curse.

You may already know that depression can cause sleep problems. If you are depressed, you may wake up very early, feel agitated, and not be able to go back to sleep. In other words, some stress in your life is triggering depression and your mind wakes you early to help you get up and deal with that stress. In this case, the depression is *primary*, that is, it comes first, and the sleep problem is *secondary*.

But the opposite can happen. You may be confronted with a problem sleeping that is a primary problem, perhaps because of travel, or stress, or life worries. You get into a bad sleep pattern, feel tired and lethargic, and begin to feel irritable. Before long, you find yourself drifting into a depression. The future looks bleak, you think of yourself in a more negative way, and the world seems unfriendly, even hostile. Now the sleep problem is primary and the depression is secondary.

YOU WOULD EXPECT that successful treatment of depression would relieve sleep problems. That turns out to not be true. When we effectively treat depression, the sleep problem can remain. Insomnia seems to take on a life of its own. We need to treat insomnia in addition to treating depression. Psychotherapy is just as effective as medication at treating depression, and it is much better at reducing the danger of relapse. Part of that effective treatment is to help patients become skilled sleepers.

THERE IS ONE TYPE OF DEPRESSION in which the patient sleeps much longer than usual – bipolar disorder. This condition is characterized by episodes of deep depression and then episodes (generally shorter) of the opposite, excitement and very high energy, usually associated with impulsive action and poor judgment. During the periods of high energy and poor judgment, the patient sleeps very little. If you have seen this pattern in yourself (sleeping longer when depressed and very short time when excited), please consider a visit to a specialist to get your condition assessed.

WHAT CAN BE DONE?

Can we learn to sleep better? When we think about improving sleep, patients may think of taking a medication to help them sleep. While these are helpful, I don't encourage them. There are problems both with the prescription sleep aids and with the over-the-counter sleep medications, as you'll see in Chapter Ten. But there is good news.

Sleep experts agree that a change in your behavior is the best treatment for sleep. In other words, good sleep is nothing but a set of habits, and we can change our habits. We can improve our sleep through learning and practicing *sleep hygiene.* That means habits that foster better sleep. In a way, we are helping you remember how to sleep well, for there was a time when you did. As a baby, as a young child, you did sleep soundly. Let's bring back those innocent and excellent childhood sleep habits.

HOW COMMON ARE SLEEP PROBLEMS?

There is a common myth that we can teach our brains to get by on less sleep without any problems. That is false. We now know that the adult human brain requires at least seven hours of sleep a night to function at its best. You can't cheat Mother Nature!

According to the National Institute of Health, the average adult in this country sleeps less than seven hours a night, and more than one-third of people are so sleep deprived that they are underperforming! They are sleepy at work, they are inattentive in social situations . . . their lack of sleep is taking a serious toll on their lives. Sleep problems are very common.

SOMETIMES OUR SLEEP PROBLEMS are a result of our own choices. We are trying to get more and more done. Although you may put off going to sleep in order to squeeze more activities into your day, eventually your need for sleep becomes overwhelming and you are forced to get some sleep. This daily drive for sleep is due, in part, to a compound known as adenosine. This natural chemical builds up in your blood as time awake adds up. While you sleep, your body breaks down the adenosine. This molecule may be what your body uses to keep track of lost sleep and to trigger sleep when needed. An accumulation of adenosine and other factors might explain why, after several nights of less than optimal amounts of sleep, you build up a sleep debt that you must make up by sleeping longer than normal. Because of such built-in molecular feedback, you can't adapt to getting less sleep than your body needs. Eventually, a lack of sleep catches up with you.

HOW ARE YOU SLEEPING?

Keep this sleep diary for four days. It will help you analyze your sleep habits. Write down the date, what time you laid down in bed, what time you got out of bed. Estimate how many minutes it took you to fall asleep. If you woke up during the night, estimate how much time you were asleep and how much time you spent awake.

HOMEWORK:

When did I go to bed? (This means, lights out!)

When did I get up in the morning?

TOTAL TIME IN BED:

How long did it take me to fall asleep?

How many times did I wake up?

How long did it take me to fall asleep if I woke up?

Total time awake after falling asleep?

TOTAL TIME ASLEEP:

Write this down <u>every day</u> for four days. This is your *baseline* sleep pattern. As you continue with this program, continue to keep this diary. Make a simple chart to track your sleep day-by-day. As you get better at sleeping skills, you should see an effect in your diary.

NOTE: On the days when you do sleep better, write down some reasons why that might be. *This part is vital. Always analyze the causes behind your successes.* Your success with this program will depend on your following this principle. Notice what works and do more of it.

For more information, go to www.SleepingSkills.com

Chapter Two

Understanding Sleep

A re we talking about a single problem here? No, to the contrary, there are many types of sleep problems, and before you tackle your sleep habits, you should understand some basic facts about sleep.

TYPES OF SLEEP

Sleep was long considered just a uniform block of time when you were not awake. Thanks to sleep studies done over the past several decades, it is now known that sleep has distinct stages that cycle throughout the night in predictable patterns. How well rested you are and how well you function depend not only on your total sleep time but on how much of the various stages of sleep you get each night.

Your brain stays active throughout sleep, and each stage of sleep is linked to a distinctive pattern of electrical activity known as brain waves. Let's review those patterns.

Sleep is divided into two basic types: rapid eye movement (REM) sleep and non-REM sleep (which has four different stages). REM means that

Before you go too far in the book, keep two or three nights of the sleep diary we suggested at the end of the first chapter. Divide the hours asleep by the hours in bed. This is *sleep efficacy*. What is your personal sleep efficacy? How long does it take you to fall asleep? Just reading this book won't cure sleep problems. Keeping the diary will help and is critical.

while you are asleep, your eyes move around, under your eyelids. REM is associated with the dream state.

Typically, sleep begins with non-REM sleep. In <u>stage 1</u> non-REM sleep, you sleep lightly and can be awakened easily by noises or other disturbances. During this first stage of sleep, your eyes move slowly, and your muscle activity slows. *Note: nearly all insomniacs spend much more time in state 1 than they think, so they believe themselves to be awake when they are actually sleeping!*

You then enter <u>stage 2</u> non-REM sleep, when your eye movements stop. Your brain shows a distinctive pattern of slower brain waves with occasional bursts of rapid waves.

When you progress into <u>stage 3</u> non-REM sleep, your brain waves become even slower, although they are still punctuated by smaller, faster waves. By <u>stage 4</u> non-REM sleep, the brain produces extremely slow waves almost exclusively. Stages 3 and 4 are considered deep sleep, during which it is very difficult to be awakened. Deep sleep is the "restorative" part of sleep that is necessary for feeling well rested and energetic during the day.

After stage 4, you typically move into REM sleep where you do most of your dreaming. During REM sleep, your eyes move rapidly in various directions, even though your eyelids remain closed. Your breathing also becomes more rapid, irregular, and shallow, and your heart rate and blood pressure increase.

During this type of sleep, your arm and leg muscles are temporarily paralyzed so that you cannot "act out" any dreams that you may be having. If you don't have this temporary paralysis, you may suffer from sleep-walking.

There is an opposite problem to sleep walking, called "hypnogogic sleep paralysis." Your mind seems to be awake, but the same paralysis is in place. This sometimes deeply frightens people, and since they are still partly asleep, they may have a very frightening dream and experience it as completely real. If it happens to you, it is an opportunity to experience something completely unusual. Understanding will help you. I experienced it once but found it interesting instead of terrifying because I knew immediately what was happening.

When people do get upset about experiencing hypnogogic sleep paralysis, they can drift into waking nightmares. They are awake and dreaming at the same time, a very unusual situation. They don't understand what is happening to them. They become afraid. Because of their fear, they feel trapped and panic. They start to dream – although they are partly awake – so their dream feels much more real, as if it is happening to them. This accounts for some of the frightening experiences people report, like being kidnaped and carried away in flying saucers. You are both awake and dreaming, so the dream feels much more real than dreams ordinarily do. So understanding what is happening will calm you.

YOUR SLEEP PATTERNS

The first period of REM sleep you experience usually occurs about an hour to an hour and a half after falling asleep. After that, the sleep stages repeat themselves continuously while you sleep. As the night progresses, REM sleep time becomes longer, while time spent in non-REM sleep stages 3 and 4 becomes shorter. By morning, nearly all your sleep time is spent in stages 1 and 2 of non-REM sleep and in REM sleep. If REM sleep is disrupted during one night, REM sleep time is typically longer than normal in subsequent nights until you catch up. You need REM sleep, and if you miss it, you will have catch up later.

Overall, almost one-half your total sleep time is spent in stages 1 and 2 non-REM sleep and about one-fifth each in

> And if tonight my soul may find her peace
> in sleep, and sink in good oblivion,
> and in the morning wake like a new-opened flower
> then I have been dipped again in God, and new-created.
> – D.H. Lawrence

deep sleep (stages 3 and 4 of non-REM sleep) and REM sleep. In contrast, infants spend half or more of their total sleep time in REM sleep. Gradually, as they mature, the percentage of total sleep time they spend in REM progressively decreases to reach the one-fifth level typical of later childhood and adulthood.

HOMEWORK: Keep up your sleep diary. Keep a running *sleep efficacy* score. Look for days when you sleep unusually well. Can you figure out what is different or unique about those nights?

Chapter Three

Diagnose Your Sleep Patterns

T here are several types of sleep problems and it is important that we help you decide which type of problem you are dealing with. Let's review them.

If your sleep problems have lasted for more than a month, you officially have a diagnosis of insomnia. Any problems lasting less than a month are considered short term. But if your insomnia lasts more than a month, it is on the road to being a chronic problem and you really ought to address it.

FALLING ASLEEP PROBLEMS

There are several reasons people cannot fall asleep. First, ask yourself whether you have a regular and healthy sleep pattern. Do you go to bed at a reasonable time? If you stay up late and then sleep in late, that plays havoc with your sleep pattern. Some people are simply "owls" who like to stay up late and sleep in late. If your job permits it, and if you get at least seven hours of sleep per night, then there is no particular harm in being an owl.

If you took my advice and have been keeping a sleep diary, you can begin to see patterns. How efficient is your sleep? If you were in bed for eight hours but only slept five, then your efficiency is 5/8, or 62.5%. Look for patterns, like sleeping better or worse on weekends, and so on.

I am not an owl, myself. I am a lark. I operate best early

in the morning and will sometimes get up at 5:30 to work on some project like this book. If you are a lark, if you are at your best early in the morning, is important that you go to sleep earlier. If you have trouble drifting off, there may be some reason you aren't falling asleep.

Do you have a quieting evening ritual? Do you turn down the lights in the evening? Do you turn down the sounds? Can you avoid watching exciting or upsetting TV programs? Perhaps you shouldn't watch any TV in the later evenings. Perhaps you will do better reading, since the brighter light coming from the television may fool your brain into thinking it is morning and not night. So you may want to avoid TV after 8:30 P.m.or so.

Part of my evening ritual is to stroll with my dogs. I walk about a mile or so, but I do not walk rapidly. Rather I enjoy the quiet time with the animals at my side. I tend to think about things I am grateful for, like living in a nice, safe neighborhood where I know many of the people well. Reviewing things I feel grateful for prepares my mind for sleep. I am content and peaceful when I settle into bed.

If you do have a problem falling asleep, then you should not watch TV in bed or read or eat in bed. For you, bed must be for sleep only or love-making and then sleep. You may have a spouse that can fall asleep in a moment, someone who can watch a very exciting TV show and then drop off to sleep as soon as the TV goes off, or even before the end of the program! So your bed becomes a TV watching place. This is not good for you.

Sometimes this difference in people will cause conflict and argument. "I don't have that problem," says a spouse, "so why do I have to suffer?" If others don't have the same problem, so what? Everyone is different. The key to a happy marriage is accepting each other's differences with some grace and compassion.

Falling asleep is helped by a quiet brain. We have good clinical evidence that when you stop thinking about the day, and instead think about comfort, peace, and relaxation, you will fall asleep quicker. That is another reason for avoiding TV as the evening grows late. The quiet brain is more likely to be a sleepy brain, and TV pushes your brain activity in the opposite direction.

Many have a "busy mind" problem. Some people fall into bed only to start replaying their whole day, worrying about possible problems in the future, or feeling grieved over past events. Of course, the brain cannot go to sleep when it is busy. In that case, you need to learn to meditate and quiet your mind. Once a day, during the daytime, meditate for at least fifteen to twenty minutes.

Generally, if you have sleep problems, you should not take daytime naps (at least not more than twenty minutes). You should meditate. Chapter Six discusses ways to meditate.

There are innumerable mental strategies for falling asleep. The common denominator is a deep quiet in the mind. If there is any worry, you won't fall asleep. You have to cure yourself of the worry habit.

THE WORRY CURE

Here is a common homework assignment for the "busy mind" problem. Early in the evening, set aside at least thirty minutes for intense worry. Try to make yourself as worried as possible, writing down all the worry thoughts you can. Sit at a table and work hard at this. Jot down your worries, and write down the "worst case scenarios." For example, you may worry about germs and getting sick. Write down the worst case scenario, such as you might die from an infection. Then write down your funeral arrangements, who would speak, who would sing, and where you wish to be buried or cremated. In other words, face your worst fears, and work through the worst that can happen.

By getting the worry "out of your system" so to speak, it becomes much easier for you to fall asleep quickly. By literally trying your best to be fearful and anxious, you face these worst fears and concerns and deal with them. You begin to master them.

It may interest you to know that by writing down worries and fears, we change our brain's reactions to them. Instead of the emotion being so overwhelming, it becomes manageable. Schedule your worry. You will be glad you did.

PROBLEMS STAYING AWAKE

One way to tell if you have a real sleep deprivation problem is to notice whether you fall asleep easily in daytime situations where you are feeling quiet and nothing is demanded of you. For example, in meetings or lectures you will see some people drifting off to sleep. That is certainly a sign of insufficient sleep. When I give talks to groups, I often see one or two who begin to doze, although my audience ratings tell me I am a very interesting speaker. You may have a similar problem. No matter how interesting the material, you may drift and doze. It is a sign you get too little quality sleep.

If you feel tired and sleepy during the day, that means you should take this sleep business very seriously, and learn better sleep habits. On the other hand, if you think you don't sleep enough but you are able to stay awake through boring meetings, perhaps you are actually getting sufficient sleep.

PROBLEMS SLEEPING TOO MUCH

Some people report very long sleep periods, ten or more hours per day. If you spend lots of time in bed and still feel tired, there is a possibility you are suffering from *sleep apnea*, a condition in which you stop breathing during the night. People with this condition never get the kind of restorative stage four sleep that they need, because they are constantly alerting themselves with breathing blockages. As they deeply relax, the back of their throat closes off and they startle themselves into much lighter sleep. Naturally they feel terribly tired during the day.

Sleep apnea is a dangerous condition. Blood pressure shoots up and the patient is not alert during the day. One study found that patients with sleep apnea are nine times more likely to have a motor vehicle accident than people with normal sleep patterns.

Here is a simple quiz to help you decide if you might have sleep apnea, developed by David White, M.D., Boston, Massachusetts:

1.Snoring
a) Do you snore on most nights (3 nights per week or more)?
    Yes (2)

No (0)

b) Is your snoring loud? Can it be heard through a door or wall?

    Yes (2)

    No (0)

2. Has it ever been reported to you that you stop breathing or gasp during sleep?

    Never (0)

    Occasionally (3)

    Frequently (5)

3. What is your collar size?

Male:

    less than 17 inches (0)

    more than 17 inches (5)

Female:

    less than 16 inches (0)

    more than 16 inches (5)

4. Do you occasionally fall asleep during the day when:

a) You are busy or active?

    Yes (2)

    No (0)

b) You are driving or stopped at a light?

    Yes (2)

    No (0)

5. Have you had or are you being treated for high blood pressure?

    Yes (1)

    No (0)

Now total up your score. Is sleep apnea a danger for you? 9 points or more: You definitely should see a sleep specialist and consider sleep studies. It is likely that sleep apnea is troubling you.

6-8 points: You should probably see a sleep specialist. You

certainly have some problems. You may or may not have sleep apnea, and only the tests a sleep specialist can give will tell you for sure.

5 points or less: It is unlikely you have sleep apnea. You may have other sleep problems, but at least apnea is unlikely.

PEOPLE WHO SLEEP MORE than nine or ten hours a day and wake up feeling completely refreshed are unlikely to even read this book. They generally see no problem with their sleep, but people around them might be jealous.

As I mentioned in Chapter One, there is a type of depression called *bipolar disorder* in which people sleep a lot when they become depressed. Sleeping more than eight hours a day, while feeling sad or down, is a possible indication of bipolar depression. This is a kind of depression that needs both medication and psychotherapy, whereas with the more typical depression (where people sleep poorly and wake up early in the morning) does equally well with either medication or psychotherapy alone. So if you feel depressed and sleep longer than usual, consider that you may have an up-and-down pattern that needs further evaluation. See a psychiatrist.

Other people who sleep too long but don't have either sleep apnea or bipolar disorder might simply have either a need or a habit of longer sleep. This is actually not particularly healthy. People who sleep longer than nine hours per night have a higher rate of death over the same time period than those who sleep seven-to-eight hours.

ONE STUDY FOUND that more than nine hours of sleep per

night or less than six are both harmful to health. Seven appears ideal for adults.

If you sleep too much, you may want to go onto a low-carbohydrate dict. There are accounts on the web of people going on the Atkins Diet, saying they used to sleep over nine hours per day and now feel great with six to seven. There are no studies at all about this, merely internet reports, so it may turn out to be meaningless.

Occasionally people sleep too much, both at night and during the day for another reason. They may have a condition called *narcolepsy*. They fall asleep suddenly or feel extremely sleepy during the day. This is often caused by poor quality nighttime sleep. You will want to see a sleep specialist for this problem.

STAYING ASLEEP

The most common complaint about sleep is not difficulty falling asleep but waking up during the night and not being able to go back to sleep. At the end of a REM cycle, you are in a very light sleep and it is not uncommon to stir and wake. If you fall asleep quickly (less than twenty minutes) there is no need to be concerned.

But if you fall asleep but then wake and lie awake and alert in the middle of night, you suffer from sleep-maintenance insomnia. This will take some detective work. There are several problems that might be causing this, and tracking down those reasons can be very helpful.

One study found that pain problems are the most common cause of sleep maintenance insomnia. If you suffer from chronic headaches, arthritis, muscle pain, then finding some relief will help a good deal. Long acting analgesics are available by prescription and may help.

Another problem is reflux disease, the stomach letting acid up into your esophagus. Other problems might include getting up to go to the bathroom, chronic cough, irritable bowel disease. Some people have Restless Leg Syndrome, and the movements will wake them up. Those are all problems that you and your doctor can grapple with.

One classic reason for midnight awakening is alcohol or drug use. Both opiate pain medication and alcohol can wake you up as they start to leave your system, generally within about three or four hours from when you take them. It is important to never use alcohol to try to go to sleep. If you can't sleep without alcohol, you might need to consider if you have an alcohol abuse problem. The cause may be your sleeplessness, but self-medicating with alcohol makes it much worse and leads to dependency.

WAKING UP EARLY

You may struggle with waking up too early. This is nearly always a case of too much thinking, either because you are depressed or you are anxious and nervous. Your thoughts are repetitive and negative as you think and worry.

The good thing about this is that your brain is trying to solve the problems that surround you. The bad

> "In every marriage there is a heavy sleeper and a light sleeper. And if two average sleepers get married, one will become heavy and one will become light."
> – Garrison Keeler

thing is that the way your brain is going about this is not going to work! We have some solutions for you for this problem.

HOMEWORK: Continue keeping your diary. Let's start the first intervention: If you don't fall asleep within twenty minutes, or you wake during the night and cannot go back to sleep in twenty minutes or less, get out of bed and do something quiet and boring, like reading a book you find uninteresting or listening to a relaxation recording. As soon as you feel sleepy, reward yourself by going back to bed. Do this for a week, see if that starts to make a difference in your sleep.

Chapter Four

Work With Your Attitude

In the opening scene of the movie *Butch Cassidy and the Sundance Kid*, some men are playing poker. A gambler says to a blond man with a moustache, "You're a pretty good card player. You haven't lost a hand since you got the deal. I'm a pretty good card player myself, and I can't figure out how you're cheating." Everyone freezes and the gambler stands up, his hand at his side, next to his gun. "The money stays, and you go," he says.

Another man rushes up to the table and tries to talk down this imminent confrontation. The gambler is resolute and repeats his demand that the blond man leave and the money stays. Finally the helpful man says to the blond man still seated at the table, "I can't help you, Sundance." The gambler blanches.

"You're the Sundance Kid?"

"They call me that."

"If I draw on you, you'll kill me."

"There is that possibility." And he slowly stands up, facing the gambler, with his hand next to his gun. The gambler now wants a way out, but is frozen in fear. The helpful man asks Sundance what it will take to let this go.

Sundance says, "He has to ask us to stay."

The two men stare at each other. The helpful man, Butch, says, "You have to ask us to stay. Come on, just ask us to stay."

"Ah . . ." says the gambler, "Can you stick around?"

"Naw," says Butch, sweeping the money into his hat, "we gotta go."

MOTHER NATURE HAS A TWISTED SENSE OF HUMOR. When we want to get rid of something, we sometimes have to relax and accept it. Being upset about being overweight, for example, raises our cortisol level which makes us more overweight. High cortisol encourages our body to store fat, so the very anxiety we feel about our weight makes us gain weight. But when we work on accepting our weight condition and nurture a sense of calm and even joy, it becomes easier for us to lose weight.

So it is with sleep. When we are troubled, we begin to worry about falling asleep. Our thinking become repetitive. "Will I sleep tonight? I hope I sleep tonight! I feel so awful when I don't sleep. I wonder if I will sleep tonight? It is just terrible when I can't sleep." On and on goes our mind, worrying about the prospect of lying awake in bed, not sleeping.

Now we have developed a habit of worry when it comes to sleep. But Mother Nature in her wisdom has decreed that worried people will not sleep! So as we work on helping you develop high quality sleep, the first thing we have to work on is attitude! We have to diagnose your habits. Do you have a habit of worry about sleep? If so, we have to change that first.

Self-talk will change worry habits. The Buddha once said, "Thoughts become attitudes, attitudes become acts, acts become habits, and habits become destiny. Take care therefore of your thoughts."

A good counter-thought method to worry is to *decatastrophize*. That means that we are going to replace alarm thoughts with hmore calming thoughts. Instead of thinking of the problem as a catastrophe, we think of it as merely inconvenient. "This is not a problem," we say to ourselves, "just an inconvenience."

Ask yourself, "How does it help me to worry and get upset about this?" After all, when we worry, we are alerting ourselves. There is a sense that something is dangerous. You wouldn't go to sleep if a dangerous criminal were prowling your neighborhood, trying to get in, would you? Then it would be healthy and smart to stay awake and alert. When you worry about whether you are going to sleep, you are doing the same thing. You are alerting yourself. You are on guard.

So firmly tell yourself, over and over, that poor sleep is not horrible, just unpleasant. It is certainly an inconvenience, but it is not a disaster or a catastrophe. Tell yourself over and over, that it is silly and pointless to worry about it. Either you will sleep or you won't but worry will not help.

Ask the insomnia to stick around. "Nah," says the insomnia, "we gotta go."

ONE TRICK INSOMNIA PLAYS ON US is to convince us that it will be awful, horrible, if we don't sleep.   Is it really so awful? No, actually when you reflect on it, we often miss sleep because of one reason or another and have to go to work the next day. It is just inconvenient, not awful. Anyone who has raised children has experienced that.

Another way to look at this is that there are actually no

catastrophes in life, only inconveniences. People go through terrible events. They are in accidents and have to live in wheelchairs. It is certainly inconvenient, but actually these people make meaningful and full lives for themselves. Some people are born with serious cerebral palsy, and their parents think of it as a catastrophe. But they can also make a full and joyful life for themselves. Consider Ricky Hoyt as an example. He was born with such severe palsy that he cannot speak or move except for some control over his head. Yet he has learned to communicate with a computer that he controls by tapping his head against a switch. He convinced his father, Rick Hoyt, to push him in a wheel chair in a five mile race. Ricky enjoyed that so much that his father began pushing him in other races, until they were able to sneak into the Boston Marathon and finish it.

If Ricky Hoyt can not only have a full life but also serve as an inspiration and help to others, why should we be concerned if we don't sleep well? It is inconvenient, but it is not a catastrophe. Don't let insomnia convince you it is a catastrophe. See it for what it is, an inconvenience.

> If some great catastrophe is not announced every morning, we feel a certain void. Nothing in the paper today, we sigh.
> – Lord Acton

HOMEWORK: Spend less, not more time in bed. Get out of bed earlier in the morning and stay up, no matter how tired you may feel. Convince yourself it will not be a catastrophe, merely unpleasant.

How early should you get up? Well, if you spend eight hours in bed, but your sleep efficiency is low, around 70%, for example, you are actually sleeping 5.6 hours per night. So reduce the time in bed to around 6 hours. Go to bed later and get up earlier.

See how that affects your sleep efficiency.

Chapter Five

Treat Your Insomnia

Now let's talk about sleep hygiene, the positive habits we want you to develop. These guidelines require a certain level of motivation so before you read this chapter, you might want to do a pro-and-con analysis. What are the advantages of doing something about your sleep? Obviously, there are many health advantages, but please try to come up with some that we haven't covered so far.

What are the disadvantages of doing something about your sleep problems? For one thing, it may be hard work. When you are already tired, it is discouraging to try something hard. There are some advantages to accepting your sleep problems and not dealing with them. Here you really want to be rather creative and exhaustive. Think of any and all reasons you may not want to deal with sleep disturbances.

Weigh each item on how important it seems, on some kind of scale, perhaps from one to three. One means it is not very important, two means it is moderately important, and three means that it is very important. Total both the Pros and the Cons of addressing your sleep problem. If the Pros do not outweigh the Cons, then we cannot recommend that you try to develop better habits, because you will not have the motivation to stick with it when it becomes difficult.

THE RULES FOR GOOD SLEEP

1:   If you do not fall asleep within twenty minutes, get out of bed and do something relaxing and distracting. For many people, this is reading. It is better to read something somewhat boring.

1a.   People are often told to not watch the clock. I have found that you *can* watch the clock, as long as you only spend twenty minutes in bed at any one time, unless you are asleep. So just make a committed decision to get out of bed if you are not asleep.

1b.   We all have things that we ought to do but don't get around to because they are unpleasant. Doing those things when you can't fall asleep will help train your brain to quickly quiet down because the unpleasant chore is waiting! Once I was trying to keep my clinical practice going and build a house at the same time. Naturally, I was a bit over-committed. I would wake up at 2:00 a.m.thinking of all the things I had to do the next day. So I instituted the twenty minute rule. My unpleasant chore was to read the Old Testament, which I had always thought I should do but found hard to enjoy. So I would stand in the bathroom reading. Very quickly I became tired. As soon as I was tired and sleepy, I rewarded myself by going right back to bed. But if I wasn't asleep in twenty more minutes, I forced myself to get out of bed again for more boring reading. Within a few days, my brain stopped waking me up.

1c   Another activity to try: Use a relaxation CD (such as the one you can order with this book – see the last page for an order form). Sit in a comfortable chair and listen to it. Return to bed as soon as you feel sleepy.

2:   Avoid housework, bills, work, or anything that is too stimulating within 2 hours of bedtime or during a nighttime awakening. Try turning off the television at least an hour before you go to bed. Do not watch TV while in bed.

A TV in the bedroom doesn't bother most people, but for someone who is prone to insomnia it is a dangerous practice. If you don't' fall asleep quickly, you may have to train your brain by dropping the lights and reducing the sounds an hour or two before you go to bed. In other words, replicate a primitive society. As night comes on, a few fires are kindled, people finish their day and sit quietly looking into the fire. A few stories are exchanged and then people go off to sleep. But if you are watching TV news or something interesting, you are flooding your brain with both too much light and with too much thought-provoking information.

3:   Although some people's insomnia is helped by a midday nap, for most, napping can interfere with falling asleep at night. The problem comes when people nap too long. They drift into deeper stages of sleep and that prevents them from falling asleep at night. Never nap for more than twenty minutes in a day. That will keep you in stage 1 sleep and you won't have the problem of a long nap disrupting your sleep architecture.

3a.   I do encourage you to *meditate* for fifteen or twenty minutes a day. Don't fall asleep, but deeply rest. It will help you be more skilled at letting go of tension quickly as you slide into bed.

3b.   I recommend *autogenic training* as a meditation skill, but *mindfulness meditation* is also excellent. In chapter six, you have a special section of autogenic training instructions for your sleep hygiene. There is a CD I mentioned on page 28 that you can order that walks you through autogenic training. You might also want to try the breathing exercise found later in this chapter. That is also on the relaxation CD.

4:   Avoid alcohol within five hours of bedtime. Alcohol is not a sleep aid because it causes nighttime awakenings. The reason for this is that alcohol does not stay in the body very long. After three or four hours, about half the alcohol you drank is metabolized.

A drug that produces relaxation when it goes into the body produces the opposite reaction when it leaves. Alcohol does relax a person as the body takes it in. So as the alcohol goes out of one's blood, the body reacts. One feels tense, nervous, and irritable. Don't use alcohol for sleep.

5:   Avoid caffeine (tea, coffee, chocolate, caffeinated soda) after noon. It can cause shallow sleep or nighttime awakenings. Insomnia patients might want to avoid caffeine altogether, even in the morning. Generally people are quite able to function without caffeine once they have weaned themselves off.

6:   Make your bedroom quiet, safe, and relaxing. Keep the bedroom as dark as possible. Light coming into the eyes is a sign for us to wake up. A hormone called *melatonin* is secreted when we are in a dark environment, and it helps us go to sleep. A lighted bedroom suppresses the melatonin.

7:   Keep consistent bedtimes and wake times seven days a week. Don't sleep in on weekends, don't stay up late to celebrate. We realize that makes us look like killjoys and there is some truth to that, but if you are prone to light sleep, it is a needful adjustment. Again, never compare yourself. You are who you are. Each person has some weaknesses to cope with in this life, and yours are not like someone else's. If you are a light sleeper, then try regulating your sleep patterns to be the same every day, and if other people aren't troubled by staying up late, good for them!

8:   Many people are victims of insomnia because they lie in bed and think and worry. There is an easy way to get around that bad habit. Schedule "worry time" earlier in the day. Use this time to resolve problems prior to bedtime. In bed remind yourself that beds are not for thinking, they are for sleeping.   Good clinical experience has shown that most insomnia is the result of a busy mind. Another way to think about this is that you have an undisciplined mind. There is an Asian saying, "The mind is a terrible master but a wonderful servant." I have found, by interviewing people who are very good sleepers, that they can turn off the "self-talk" part of the brain. What do they think about instead? They focus on the feelings in their body. They focus on how pleasant the bed feels. They focus on happy thoughts.

9:   Daily exercise improves sleep, although the effects may not be immediate. Thirty minutes is sufficient. Do not exercise within four hours of bedtime unless you find you can quickly relax and quiet your metabolism. Most people cannot, so exercise should be done before 6:30 P.m.. You may know someone who can do an energetic workout at 9:00 P.m.and fall asleep quickly at 10:30 P.m.. Good for them. If you can do that, exercise is excellent. But if you are too stimulated by exercise, you will have to adopt an exercise routine much earlier in the day.

10:   Avoid going to bed on either an empty stomach or a full stomach. A light snack may be of value. Chapter 8 discusses eating and insomnia. You may want to experiment with your eating habits.

11:   A good nighttime ritual is a to take warm bath in low light. Let the bath warm you all over and then get into bed. Natural sleep patterns include the body cooling down. By having the warm bath first and allowing your body to cool down slowly, you are triggering a nice sleep reflex.

12: Don't spend more than eight hours in bed, whether you are asleep or not. Get out of bed and go about your day, and don't nap. Catastrophic thinking will make this hard. "Oh, it will be awful if I have to get up on time even when I haven't slept," cries the "Catastrophic Thinking" part of you. Talk back to that, be strong, and get up and get going. Remember that missing sleep is not a catastrophe, just an inconvenience.

MINDFUL BREATHING

Mindful breathing helps us turn off thoughts and relax. Here is a simple exercise. Your lungs have three lobes, a bottom, a middle, and a top lobe. Visualize those three parts and as you breathe in, try to fill the bottom lobe first, then the middle, and finally the top. Now slowly exhale. Focus your attention on how the body feels while you breathe in that fashion. Breathe slowly and focus on feelings.

As you do that, you might find that your mind begins to be busy. Thoughts come to mind. Memories, or plans, or worries . . . it doesn't matter what. That is the untrained mind. Now simply say to yourself, "That's just thinking, thinking." Release those thoughts and focus clearly on the feelings of your breath flowing in and out, filling the bottom lobe, now the middle, now the top lobe of your lungs.

Again, it is likely that more thoughts will intrude. That is completely natural. Just say to yourself, "Thinking, thinking . . ." and release the thoughts. Repeat that each time thoughts well up. This is *your* time. It doesn't belong to the thinking part of your brain, it belongs to the quiet part.

Do that exercise daily for ten minutes. Each day that you do, you will find your skill is improving. Each night as you retire, you find you can focus more fully on the *feelings* of settling down into your bed. Learn from the good sleepers and relish the feeling of lying down. Nurture a happy reaction to slipping into your bed. "Oh, I love my bed," says the good sleeper. And because she loves it, she benefits from it.

COMMENTS ON EXERCISE AND LIGHT

Most insomnia sufferers should not exercise at night. A

workout within two hours of bed will, for some, energize rather than relax them. Yet regular exercise is certainly an aid for good sleep. What can be done?

While people may exercise harder when they do it at night, when they exercise in the morning or at noon they tend to stick with it better. Scheduling your exercise in the morning or at noon might be just the pattern for you. If you are already good at exercise, the next paragraph is not for you. But if you are not such a fan of physical fitness, let me pose a question. What is the ideal form of exercise?

It takes the least amount of equipment, it is easiest to fit into your daily life, and it is something that most of us have done since we were one year old. I am talking about walking.

A thirty minute walk once a day can sometimes provide the kind of stress relief and gentle exercise that helps people sleep. If you go late in the day or early evening, you might try a stroll, not a vigorous walk. In other words, saunter along as if you have all the time in the world. It is very relaxing.

There is some evidence that people who wake up in the middle of the night may benefit from light therapy. That is, humans have moved from a life that is predominantly outdoors to one that is predominantly indoors. We no longer work or live outdoors.

For example, perhaps a hundred years ago people might sit on their porches at evening time, to talk with neighbors, sing and tell stories with family, and so forth. This outdoor exposure may have helped quiet the mind; certainly the socializing did. From time immemorial humans flourished with face-to-face connection. But now we sit indoors, stare at a bright screen where there are figures that resemble humans but don't interact with us. We have become a world of peepers, watching but not connecting.

So if deep, uninterrupted sleep is what you are after, how about trying a noontime walk? That gives you the natural outdoor sunlight and low-impact exercise. If a noontime walk is simply out of the question, try a light box. You can find many companies selling 10,000 lux therapy lights on the internet. You need to spend at least 30 minutes a day in close proximity to the light.

You do not have to look directly at the light; you can read books, for example. But you do have to let that light flood into your eyes, even if you aren't looking directly at the light. Experiencing that full-spectrum light that mimics the natural sunlight is vital.

You see, there is a hormone called melatonin that helps the body get used to cycles of morning and night. When you look at bright light during the day, the melatonin washes out of your body, and when the daylight fades and the evening comes on, the melatonin rises in your body, signaling you that it is time to get ready for bed. Melatonin doesn't make you sleepy so much as tells you when it is time to be sleepy. So regular light and dark are very important.

> "If a man had as many ideas during the day as when he has insomnia, he'd make a fortune."
> – Griff Niblack

HOMEWORK: Make a checklist out of the sleep

habit suggestions in this chapter. Rate yourself each day as to how well you are accomplishing them. Check your progress with your diary. How is your sleep efficiency number? Does it reflect good progress?

If your sleep efficiency is 85% or more, add fifteen minutes to your total bedtime sleep per week. That is, if you are now spending six hours in bed, but your sleep efficiency has improved to 85%, then spend six hours and fifteen minutes in bed. Each time your sleep efficacy is 85% or more, reward yourself with fifteen minutes more time in bed.

Chapter Six

What About Naps?

W hat do Leonardo da Vinci, Napoleon, Winston Churchill, and John Kennedy all have in common? They were all devoted to the concept of power naps, a short rest taken after lunch.

Most sleep researchers discourage naps. This is because too many people who nap actually sleep too long. The idea is that if you slip into stage 3 or 4 sleep, you will disrupt your nighttime sleep patterns and make your insomnia problems worse. Furthermore, when you try to wake up from a longer nap, and you have been in deeper sleep stages, you will feel very lethargic and disoriented. This may last for some time. Paradoxically you don't feel as rested because you are fighting with the brain's pattern of staying asleep for hours, once the stage 4 sleep is reached. So long daytime naps are certainly not a good idea.

If you can limit your nap time to around twenty minutes, you will stay in stage 1 sleep and feel much better. There is some research indicating that people taking a short nap of around twenty minutes reduce their risk of heart disease when compared with people who never nap. People who take these "power naps" are much more productive and energized the rest of the afternoon.

DAILY MEDITATION

I actually recommend something slightly different. A beneficial, positive practice is to meditate every day for twenty minutes, preferably right after lunch. There are so many positive studies of meditation that we can say without fear of contradiction that everyone should meditate. Those who meditate every day have better immune systems, better heart health, are more creative and insightful, are more peaceful and less reactive to sudden noises.

Meditation is the art of quieting the brain. Since most people who suffer from insomnia have an over-active brain, mediation is an ideal discipline.

There are many ways to meditate. The style I will teach you, *Autogenic Training*, was developed by physicians in Germany. It is not better or worse than any other style, it is simply one approach.

Another approach is Mindfulness Meditation which was developed from Buddhism. Jon Kabat-Zinn has three books on Mindfulness Meditation: *Wherever You Go, There You Are*, *Full Catastrophe Living* and *The Mindful Way through Depression*.

Still another discipline is meditation on a *mantra* or a short phrase. The discipline is: you repeat or chant the mantra to yourself for twenty minutes. Most teachers suggest you do this silently, in your mind. You simply sit comfortably in a chair. When your mind wanders away from the mantra, patiently return to chanting the mantra. The goal is to be able to chant the mantra to yourself for the full twenty minutes, during which the mind is deeply at rest.

Transcendental Meditation (TM) uses mantras in the Sanskrit language, such as *au nam* or *om mani padi hum*. The TM belief is that these Sanskrit mantras have unique qualities because of their sounds.

Do the sounds in mantras have special power? There is no evidence for this whatsoever. Dr. Herbert Benson at Harvard has studied mantra meditation and found it very helpful for producing the *relaxation response*. But the special mantras didn't matter. He used the mantra, *Coca-Cola* and found it worked as well as the "magical" Sanskrit mantras. But he also found something more. Inspiring mantras help most. "Holy Spirit brings peace" might be a good choice for religious people. Use a short phrase that would suggest peace, gratitude, and love.

Many types of meditation are helpful. Because I was taught Autogenic Training, that is what I teach, but you can easily find teachers who will help you learn mantra or mindfulness or many other styles. What they all have in common is to discipline the mind to a quiet, restorative state.

AUTOGENIC TRAINING

These autogenic training exercises can help you recover from anxiety, stress, and tension. In this style of meditation you will repeat a series of phrases in English.

Repeat every phrase, silently, in your mind, *three times*. Say the phrase in a quiet, thoughtful way. Pause after the phrase for a few seconds and notice how you feel. Focus on your feelings for two or three breaths.

Practice at least twice a day: once during the day and then again as you lie down to sleep. The more often you return your body to a state of restful quiet, the more energy and self control you will experience.

A patient who had a painful condition of irritable bowel syndrome found she had to practice five times a day. When she did, the cramping and other symptoms went away. She would practice for about ten minutes before going to work, at her morning break, at lunch, at her afternoon break, and again when she came home from work. Her delight at completely eliminating the symptoms made all her practice well worthwhile.

Read through all the phrases and get an idea of how they fit together. Try to master Set 1 first, then Sets 1 and 2, then Sets 1, 2, and 3, and so on. At the end of each practice session, take a deep breath, stretch, and open your eyes. Say to yourself, "Alert and awake."

Set 1:

I feel quite quiet . . .   I am easily relaxed . . .

My right arm feels heavy and relaxed . . . My left arm feels heavy and relaxed . . . My arms feel heavy and relaxed . . . My right leg feels heavy and relaxed . . . My left leg feels heavy and relaxed . . . My arms and legs feel heavy and relaxed . . .

My hips and stomach are quiet and relaxed . . . My breathing is calm and regular . . . My heartbeat is calm and peaceful . . . My shoulders feel heavy . . . My face is smooth and quiet . . .I am beginning to feel quite relaxed. . .

Set 2:

My right hand is warm . . . Warmth flows into my right hand . . . My left hand is warm . . . Warmth flows into my left hand . . . My hands are warm . . . Warmth flows into my hands . . . My right foot is warm . . . My left foot is warm . . . My hands and feet are warm . . . Warmth flows into my

hands and feet . . . (As you breathe in, imagine the cool are flowing up through you forehead, cooling the forehead, and say:) My forehead is cool . . . (As you exhale, imagine warm are flowing around your eyes, warming the eyes, and say:) My eyes are warm . . . My forehead is cool and my eyes are warm . . . I am warm and peaceful . . .
(Continue the "forehead cool, eyes warm" pattern for several minutes.)

Set 3:

I am beginning to feel quite relaxed . . . My bed is for sleep or rest . . . I don't have to think about anything in bed . . . I do not have to remember anything . . . I do not have to plan anything . . . Beds are for sleep . . . Beds are for sleep, not for thinking . . . I appreciate the break from thinking . . . I am glad to take a break from thinking . . . I appreciate myself when I rest . . .

Set 4:

My breathing is calm and regular. . . My heartbeat is calm and regular. . . I am at peace. . . Sounds and sights around contribute to peace. . . Peace goes with me though out the day . . . There is nothing to bother and nothing to disturb. . . My mind is very quiet . . . There is nothing to think about now . . . My mind is quiet . . .

Set 5:

Rest is good for me . . . I feel good about resting deeply . . . Whether I sleep or rest, I am pleased . . . I can cope very well with deep rest . . . I am able to cope whether I sleep or just rest . . . There is nothing to bother or disturb me . . . Nothing can harm or disturb me now . . .

I am not required to think . . . I don't have to think now . . . Thoughts are not important now . . . There is nothing to bother or disturb me now . . . There is nothing to remember now . . . There is nothing to plan now . . . My bed is for comfort and not for thinking . . . I feel pleased with my bed . . . I feel comfortable in my bed . . . I feel grateful for my bed . . . I notice the comfort of my bed . . .

Sleep-time Application

You will want to practice Autogenic Training during the day for at least a week or two. If you achieve consistent restorative rest you are ready to apply it at night. Now when you are lying in bed, you can review the autogenic training skills. Arms heavy, legs heavy, hands warm, feet warm. Tell yourself, "Beds are for sleep, not for thinking . . . There is nothing to think about now . . . there is nothing to remember . . . there is nothing to plan . . . thinking is not important now . . ." and so on.

CHRONIC PAIN RELIEF

Suppose pain such as arthritis interferes with your sleep? I have used the following process myself and found it quite helpful in relieving pain. I have also used it with many, many patients who have found great relief. As you achieve good heaviness in the arms and legs and warmth in the hands and feet, follow this process:

1. On a scale from one to ten, rate your current pain. One is no pain at all and ten is the worst pain you have ever had.

Now picture this number on a card. Let the card move away from you, getting farther and farther away. Finally, it is so far away that you can no longer see it.

2. What color is the pain? Imagine your awareness could float outside of your body and look with a kind of X-ray vision. See the pain as a color in your body. Now imagine you have a healing liquid in a sprayer, and you gently wash the pain away. Wash away, rinse away that color and see the healthy tissue begin to emerge. Keep washing away the pain / color until you can see nothing but healthy tissue.

3. Now imagine the pain is a quantity of liquid. It is in a container in front of you. Reach over and open a valve at the bottom and feel the liquid run out. Put your fingers under the valve and feel the liquid run out. Feel it and ask yourself about its qualities. It the liquid warm or cool? Oily or watery? Thick or thin and runny? Slippery or sticky?

Keep your hand under that liquid and let it run over the fingers. Imagine a drain where the liquid runs away. Notice the pain turning to a thin stream, to a dribble, to a drip, to a slow drip. Wait until the liquid stops running.

4. Now suppose the pain were a sound. What would it sound like? Imagine you can slowly change the sound. Perhaps by turning knobs, you can change the qualities of the sound. Experiment with changing the sound.

If the sound were a voice, what might it say to you? If you could discuss what the pain is trying to do for you, what questions would you ask the pain?

When you have some comfort with the sound, move back to the number rating. What rating would you give the pain now? See the number in front of you and push it away from yourself. Repeat the whole sequence at least three times.

> "The best cure for insomnia is to get a lot of sleep."
> – W. C. Fields

HOMEWORK: Practice 15 - 20 minutes of meditation each day and track your sleep efficiency.

Chapter Seven
A Snoring Cure?

I found camping with a particular friend painful. He would snore all night, loudly, and keep me awake. Out of desperation, I invented a nighttime process he could use to stop his snoring, and I taught it to him. It worked (much to his wife's delight), and since then I have taught it to a few clients. It works quite well.

Bear in mind that snoring might be a sign of sleep apnea, and we don't want that to go untreated. You ought to have a serious snore evaluated. But if you snore but are not suffering from sleep apnea, this might work for you.

To do a good job of this, you will have to do some work. The first thing to do is to collect some information on how your sleep is right now. Ask your spouse to rate your snoring each night and keep a graph.

Rate your sleep quality for each night's sleep. Every morning, rate how rested you feel; rate how quiet your bed-partner reports you were. Use a 1 - 10 rating scale, with 10 being negative ratings, and 1 equaling ideal. Rate average as 5 or 6; five slightly better than average, and six as slightly worse than average.

To help make sense of these two types of data on the chart, use symbols to rate the different aspects. Use the following symbols: a circle and a star. Connect each one to form a line graph.

O---O   1: SLEEP QUALITY: (1 = I feel completely rested; 10 = I feel terrible, no rest at all.)

☆---☆   2:QUIET SLEEP: (spouse rates you as:1= totally quiet, 10 = as loud as you have ever been.)

Please graph <u>data</u> for every day!

10 worst!															
9															
8															
7															
6 average +															
5 average															
4 average -															
3															
2															
1 Best!															
Date (dd/mm)															

After you have a few nights of data, start to train yourself to not snore. This is easily done. It will be very important that you have practiced the Autogenic Training in the last chapter.

We have more capacity to control ourselves while asleep than you would imagine. Psychologists have shown that you can practice a behavior while awake - such as scratching your nose when you hear a certain sound - and then while asleep, you will actually scratch your nose when the sound occurs, even though you don't consciously hear it.

In a sense, we all know this. Most of us have made up our minds to wake up at a certain time for a special event (like,

going fishing with friends at 5:00a.m.) and then we awake
before the alarm clock goes off! A new mother might be
exhausted from caring for the newborn infant. She will sleep
through a chorus line singing and dancing in her bedroom.
But if the baby starts to whimper, that same mother awakens!
How did she know that sound was relevant, while other
sounds were not? Clearly some part of our mind does
monitor our behavior without our conscious awareness.

Snoring is caused by too much muscle relaxation in the
throat area. Many people snore because the muscles in their
soft palette become overly relaxed and begin to vibrate.
Some doctors will scar that muscle to keep it more toned
during sleep, and that scaring treatment does work. But there
is a much simpler answer. To stop snoring you only have to
rehearse a slight muscle tension when the snoring begins. It is
not very hard.

In the following exercise, it is of great importance that
you relax deeply, *but* you are not to fall asleep. This exercise
only takes five minutes or so. Please be sure to stay awake
until the exercise period is over.

HERE'S WHAT YOU WILL DO: Lie on your back in bed. Relax
deeply all over. Concentrate on deeply relaxing the throat.
Breathe deeply and regularly, and relax until you actually feel
your throat start to restrict.

That is the beginning of your snoring habit. Now, *while
you stay completely relaxed in the rest of your body*, open the
throat. Keep the throat opened up for a couple of minutes.
You have begun to train your throat to immediately stop the

snore.

Repeat this process four more times. Let the snore just begin and then open the throat. Keep breathing deeply and slowly, a sleep style of breathing.

Now spend about a minute simply relaxing and keeping the air flowing silently. Keep the throat opened up and repeat to yourself:

"At the first sign of a snore, my throat automatically opens up and stays open."

Think that thought in your mind while you focus on the feelings of effortless breathing.

Please study carefully and thoughtfully your physical sensations. What does it feel like when you stop the snore?

Are you able to stay physically completely relaxed and comfortable while you stop the snore?

Is the rest of your body deeply relaxed?

It is helpful for you to reflect on how the throat feels while you are breathing freely and effortlessly. Throughout the day, recall that feeling, and emphasize the awareness to yourself.

Now graph the quality / quietness of your sleep with the same graph. Are you getting better sleep? Is your sleep more quiet?

Keep that work up until you are sure you have conquered snoring.

SLEEP APNEA AND CPAP

People with sleep apnea may need to rely on Continuous Positive Airway Pressure, or CPAP. Without that, they are literally suffocating during the night, and are in great danger of feeling terribly un-rested, sleepy during the day, not alert, and so on.

Yet many patients find the CPAP mask that fits tightly over the nose and mouth intolerable.

If you are one of these, you can re-program yourself to accept the CPAP, using Autogenic Training (AT).

Practice your AT every day. Add these phrases, repeating each phrase three times:

"When I notice the CPAP mask, I remember to relax . . . the feeling of the CPAP mask reminds me to relax . . . The feeling of the mask makes me relax . . . When I feel the mask, I relax and feel peaceful . . . I remember to feel grateful for the mask . . . I am grateful the mask helps me breathe . . . I feel grateful and peaceful with the mask . . . The mask makes me relaxed, peaceful, and sleepy . . . With the mask I feel sleepy and peaceful . . ."

As you program yourself, recall the physical feeling of the mask being in place.

After a few days of that mental training using those phrases, do the same training but this time with the mask actually in place. Repeat the whole series of phrases two or three times with the mask in place.

You may have to do this once, or you might have to renew training each night. Each person is different.

At breakfast, an hour ago, I ventured, for the first time, to throw out a feeler, for all these days' silence made me a little uneasy and suspicious. I intimated that at home, I sometimes snored--not often, and not much, but a little--but it might be possible that at sea, I--though I hoped--that is to say--But I was most pleasantly interrupted at that point by a universal outburst of compliment and praise, with assurances that I made the nights enjoyable for everybody, and that they often lay awake hours to listen, and Mr. Rogers said it infused him with so much comfortableness that he tried to keep himself awake by turning over and over in bed so as to get more of it; Rice said it was not a coarse and ignorant snore, like some people's, but was a perfectly gentlemanly snore; Colonel Payne said he was always sorry when night was over and he knew he had to wait all day before he could have some more; and Tom Reed said the reason he moved down into the coal bunkers was because it was even sweeter, there, where he could get a perspective on it. This is very different from the way I am treated at home, where there is no appreciation of what a person does.

– Samuel Clemens, Letter to Olivia Clemens, August 9, 1901, reprinted in Mark Twain's Correspondence with Henry Huttleston Rogers

HOMEWORK: If you snore or use CPAP, try this program. Using your Autogenic Training skills, improve your sleeping behavior. Track your results.

Chapter Eight

Diet and Sleep

C an changing your diet help you sleep better? I find it is useful, although not too important. Diet can play a role in whether you sleep well or not. So let's review a few principles that you can experiment with.

BEST DIET RULE EVER

"Eat like a king at breakfast and a pauper at supper." So let's start with that. Have a good breakfast. I suggest whole wheat or whole grains at breakfast, along with a healthy fat source.

For example: One-half cup of oatmeal, a cup of fruit (such as strawberries or blueberries) cooked into the oatmeal, along with a generous tablespoon of chopped walnuts. Some people don't like their fruit cooked, but I do, so I cook them all together.

Top with some skim milk or low-fat yogurt. Add an omelet with sauteed vegetables for a meal that stays with you all morning.

Similar breakfast choices would emphasize whole grain cereals and healthy fats. The healthy fats are found in nuts and seeds, such as pumpkin seeds. They are fats that help our brain and body to function at its best. The Japanese eat fish for breakfast. When I was in Japan, I tried it, and it is not bad at all.

Flax seeds are a particularly good sources of the healthy fats. They are actually the best of all seeds and nuts. Your body will not digest them, though, unless you grind them up.

You can buy a small seed grinder, like a coffee grinder, and zap the seeds, breaking their tough shell so your body can access the healthy fats. I don't really like the flax seed taste but I still use them, sprinkling a couple of tablespoons on my cereal in the morning.

Lunch: Eat your main protein source along with plenty of vegetables. For example, a chicken breast with two or three steamed or sauteed vegetables and a piece of whole-grain bread. The "Mediterranean Diet" is the most healthy way we know to eat, and it emphasizes large salads and healthy (non-animal) fats. Olive oil or canola oil are healthy fats. The best animal sources of fats are fish, especially deep ocean fish. The best is Alaska salmon, because it is against the law in Alaska to raise salmon in pens. This guarantees that the salmon are wild-caught and contain the healthy Omega-3 fatty acids. People who eat high levels of Omega-3s are calmer and more peaceful and often report they sleep better.

Nearly all animals we eat are not good sources of healthy fats, and we ought to avoid eating them. There is an exception. If you could find chickens fed on greens and flax seeds, their meat would be good. Eggs advertised as "Omega-3" are widely available. The chickens have been fed a flax seed diet and produce much healthier eggs. Chickens raised in pastures also produce healthier eggs, because of the grass they eat. You can find them at some Farmers Markets.

Another exception is "grass-fed beef." A cow that has only eaten grass, never fed grains, is just as healthy for you as deep ocean fish. If you google "grass fed beef" plus your state or city, you will find ranchers who sell beef that have

never been fed corn. Look at my friends at
www.bar10beef.com, for one example.

Grass-fed beef is more expensive. Are you worth it? Like
ocean fish, grass fed beef have the Omega-3 oils ("essential
fatty acids") that have many benefits. Several studies have
shown that Omega-3 fatty acids reduces hyperactivity and
depression. Certainly the Omega-3 oils reduce heart attack
and stroke risk, so they are worthwhile for that reason alone.

The general rule is "fewer legs, better health" when it
comes to eating. Chicken, turkey, other fowl are better than
beef and pork that you buy in a typical supermarket; and fish
is better than fowl.

Dinner: Go light! Eat small portions, and at least two or
three vegetables. For example: A small portion, two ounces,
of meat or fish, two or three vegetables (½ cup of steamed
spinach with a bit of vinegar, steamed summer squash, some
broccoli with soy sauce, peas, and so on) and a half a baked
potato. Salads are great for filling up without overeating. Top
your salad with two tablespoons of olive oil and one
tablespoon of balsamic vinegar.

Nighttime snack: Eat lightly before bed, emphasizing
carbohydrates. Heavy protein at night keeps your body
working hard and will give you restless sleep. For example,
two graham crackers and six ounces of skim milk; a banana
and a small glass of skim milk, or perhaps whole wheat toast
and yogurt. Eating more usually results in disturbed sleep.

Often people like to warm up their milk before bed.
When it was available, I used to drink Postum made with hot

milk instead of water. If you don't know, Postum was a toasted wheat drink, a caffeine-free substitute for coffee. Kraft Foods discontinued it to the dismay of the very small but loyal group of fans. What about hot chocolate? The problem with hot chocolate is that it contains caffeine, and you want to avoid that at night. So Postum fit the bill. Health food stores still have similar coffee substitutes.

A new study from Spain, which followed over 10,000 persons for more than four years, found that the Mediterranean diet does prevent depression. Those Spaniards who closely followed their traditional diet were thirty percent less likely to suffer a depressive episode during the four and a half years they were studied. What was the traditional diet? Fish instead of beef, less bread, more legumes, vegetables, nuts, seeds, and olives, and olive oil.

A flock of sheep that leisurely pass by
One after one; the sound of rain, and bees
Murmuring; the fall of rivers, winds and seas,
Smooth fields, white sheets of water, and pure sky -
I've thought of all by turns, and still I lie
Sleepless...
    – William Wordsworth, "To Sleep"

HOMEWORK: How does a shift in eating the Mediterranean diet affect your sleep?

Chapter Nine

Putting It All Together

Now we have a complete strategy for better sleep. Let's put it into play. Creating the best conditions for sleep does take some effort. The question of motivation is a curious one, although people with insomnia problems feel motivated to change, when I ask them to try out good sleep discipline habits, the "sleep hygiene" rules, they find it hard to do it. When we are tired, our best intentions often fade and we do the opposite of what we had planned to do.

We need some special techniques to actually make changes in habits, especially the habits to do with sleep.

QUIET THE MIND

First, are you training your brain to quiet down? Are you practicing some form of meditation? Do you do it every day? People who taketwentyminutes in the middle of the day to meditate and quiet the mind can call on those skills when they go to bed. Very good clinical experience tells us that sleep problems can be caused by *sub-vocalizing* or in other words, self-talk. Relaxing the mind helps. Try quieting statements as you find in the Autogenic Training. I like to emphasize "There is nothing to remember now. There is nothing to plan now. I am not required to think about anything now."

Take twenty minutes during the day. It is a great investment of your effort, and will pay off. If you are not doing it, try to diagnose your state of motivation.

THE MOTIVATION ASSESSMENT

Rate your motivation to change with two questions: (1) Is the proposed change <u>important to me</u>? Rate "importance" on a 0 - 10 scale, with zero meaning it is not at all important, and ten meaning it is the highest importance possible. (2) Is the change I am thinking of something I am <u>confident I can do</u>? Use the same 0 - 10 rating scale.

If you rate the change as low in "importance" but high in "confidence" then you may want to do a pro-and-con analysis as we mentioned in Chapter Five. Simply divide a paper into two columns, and write down all the changes you'd expect to see, with the positive changes on one side and the negative changes, the costs, on the other side.

DOING AUTOGENIC TRAINING EVERY DAY

PRO	CON
It might help me sleep	It interrupts my day
Maybe be more productive?	People at work think I'm weird
I am tired of sleep problems	I doubt it will really work
???	???

Rate how important each of these items are for you, on a three point scale: one means "not at all important," two means "somewhat important," and three means "very important." Total each side. Which has the greater weight? That is your decision.

If you rate change as high in importance and low in confidence, use this chapter to raise your confidence rating.

BEDS ARE FOR SLEEPING, NOT LYING THERE

Do you get up if you aren't asleep in twenty minutes? It feels better to lie in bed than get up. But if you continue to lie in bed, you are teaching your brain to be active while in bed. You are not giving yourself a consequence. So now your bed becomes a place you associate with futile effort. That is not what you want. The bed should be a place where you enjoy settling in. It should be a place associated in your mind with quickly falling asleep. That is why you get up after twenty minutes.

Of course, you should go right back to bed as soon as you feel any tiredness and sleepiness. But if you aren't asleep in twenty minutes, it is out of bed again! Do a chore until you feel sleepy. As an alternative to a chore, you might sit in a comfortable chair and listen to a relaxation audio, such as the relaxation CD that you can order in the back of the book. Then you reward yourself for feeling sleepy by allowing your body to rest in your bed.

As you get into bed, pause. Think about how good it will feel to slide down between the sheets. As you do settle into bed, focus on good feelings. Consciously let all your muscles relax. Smile to yourself as you notice good feelings.

DEALING WITH FEARS

What might get in your way? Fears, for one thing. "If I get out of bed, I will be even more tired and exhausted tomorrow morning. It will be awful." Make sure you have adjusted your attitude so that you see sleeplessness as simply an inconvenience, not a disaster.

If the room feels cold, slip on a warm robe and get up anyway.

HEALTHY EATING

Make sure your eating habits support good sleep, with Omega-3 oils present and a healthy pattern of meals. Eat well, exercise, and practice moderation.

SCHEDULE WORRY

If you find your mind buzzing at night, be sure you are scheduling a half hour of worry time every day. Write down your worries and describe the very worst thing that can happen and how you would survive it. If the worst thing is your own death, plan out your funeral.

Related to this, some folks find great comfort in keeping a daily journal. It helps them figure out what might be bothering them if they don't already know. It is also a good place to list good things that happen to them, so they can review what they are grateful for as they lie in bed.

SOME OTHER TOOLS

Shifting from self-talk to visualizing helps some people. For example, imagine you are constructing a cabin in the woods. Dig the foundations, lay foundation stones, grout them with concrete, chop and peel logs . . . Many patients report they fall asleep quickly when they do this.

Breathing exercises: Breathe in to a count of three and out to a count of six. Count the number of breaths.

Count your breaths in sets of four. Count ONE, two, three, four, TWO, two, three, four, THREE, two, three, four, FOUR, two, three, four, FIVE, two, three, four . . . and so on.

Relaxation CDs are widely available. Use one when you get up to remind yourself of how to relax.

You can purchase a Galvanic Skin Response (GSR) feedback unit. A company in Canada offers them for around one hundred dollars ("Thought Technology, Inc."). If you aren't asleep in twenty minutes, get up, sit in a comfortable chair, and use the GSR feedback to train yourself in very deep relaxation.

With all these tools, honor the twenty minute rule.

CASE EXAMPLES

Aaron (all names are changed) complained he would wake during the night and feel very alert and agitated. He did not find listening to the CD helpful. He purchased a galvanic skin response (GSR) biofeedback unit for roughly the cost of a single psychotherapy session. The GSR produces a tone which changes when the person relaxes. Aaron practiced with the unit during the day until he was able to reduce the tone. When he woke up during the night, he sat in a comfortable recliner and attached the GSR to his fingers and relaxed. He was able to return to bed within twenty minutes and fell asleep quickly. After a few weeks, he was not waking up any more.

Barbara found it hard to fall asleep. She complained that random worry thoughts ran through her head when she lay down. While practicing meditation during the day did help somewhat, her breakthrough came when she began setting

aside a "worry time" where she would write down all the
worries she could think of. She practiced intensive worry for
thirty minutes each afternoon.

At night, she agreed to spend no more than twenty
minutes awake in bed. If she was not asleep, she got up and
reviewed her worry work. Her therapist suggested that she
take each worry to an ultimate conclusion and then practice
acceptance of that outcome. She objected, "What if the worst
conclusion is that I would die?" Her therapist asked her, "Do
you think you will not? All of us die, and the wise accept it."

She practiced an accepting attitude, telling herself that
death is not a catastrophe, only an inconvenience. "I'd rather
live longer," she affirmed, "but death comes to all, early or
late. Dying early is only inconvenient." Her minor worries
were no problem. Her sleep improved.

Charlie was also distracted when he went to bed. He
benefitted from focusing on the sensations of his bed, rather
than on his thoughts. He reviewed every part of his body and
how the bed felt. How did the bed feel to his knees, for
example? How about his hips? What about the comfort of the
pillow?

He practiced sliding into bed and immediately focusing
on sensations. He found that within twenty minutes he was
asleep.

Della could not quiet her mind, no matter what tools her
therapist offered. Finally she found a combination of two
skills helped. First, she practiced the focus on sensations.
That was somewhat helpful. Then she tried to impose a
strong rule on herself while in bed. "I must not close my
eyes," she affirmed, "until I am asleep." This task gave her

something to think about, and she was paradoxically trying hard to keep her eyes awake while at the same time relaxing with the focus on sensations. It worked.

Elaine found that awakening early was her biggest problem. She would wake up around 4:30 a.m. and was unable to fall back asleep. Her therapist suspected a mild depression was present, since early awakening is one of the symptoms. She began a gratitude diary. Before going to bed, she would write down five small things that she was grateful for that day. She wrote about how they came about and how they helped her. This project yielded a very profitable return. Not only did Elaine fall asleep more quickly, but she found she awoke with a much improved mood. Instead of waking up early, she slept a normal number of hours.

Gary found something rather surprising. He had been having large evening snacks, so he agreed to have a very light snack. That improved his sleep, and he tried skipping his snack and going to bed a bit hungry. Unlike many people, he found that he actually fell asleep much better with a bit of hunger. He even experimented with going to bed without any supper, and to the surprise of both him and his therapist, he slept even better. Of course, he also found he lost weight.

Hamish was a teen who had unknowing reset his biological clock. He slept in every day and didn't attend high school. Mother Nature doesn't mind if you stay up late, which teens love to do anyway, and will allow you to add time at the other end. He was staying up later and later until he was going to bed at 3:00 a.m. after playing computer games with other teens around the world. Naturally he slept until noon, and his parents, who were following a laissez-faire approach of letting him raise himself, didn't interfere. Instead they took him to a shrink to do what they were unwilling to do, help Hamish order his life.

Hamish actually did want to go to school and graduate, and wasn't punishing his parents for their lack of love (although they did deserve it). If we told Hamish to simply go to bed at 10:30 p.m., however, he would lie awake, his mental clock telling him that bedtime was hours off yet. The body doesn't like to push the biological clock backwards.

Instead, we push the clock forward. We petitioned the school for a few days of absence while Hamish was treated for a serious sleep disorder. He agreed to a treatment protocol. Hamish went to bed three hours later each day. The first day, he went to bed at 5:00 a.m., and slept as long as he wanted. The next day, it was 8:00 a.m., then 11:00 a.m., then 2:00 p.m., and continued that until he reached 10 p.m., staying up only two hours later that night. He then agreed to wake at 6:00 a.m. each day and returned to school and was able to finish his classes and graduate.

Inez used *sleep deprivation therapy*. She suffered from *sleep fragmentation*. She woke multiple times during the night, and her sleep efficacy was about 5/8, or 62.5%. That means she was actually sleeping only five of the eight hours she was in bed. Desperate to sleep better, she agreed to something very difficult. She only allowed herself to spend five hours a day in bed. When she felt tired, she would go to bed, but she had to set an alarm clock to wake up five hours later. So if she went to bed at 10:00 p.m., she was up by 3:00 a.m..

As soon as she slept soundly all five hours, with no

waking during that block of time, she allowed herself to sleep a bit longer, increasing her time in bed by fifteen minutes, and keeping that additional time only if she slept soundly the entire time. Her sleep fragmentation disappeared.

Julie heard of recent studies that found that practicing yoga helped people sleep better. She enrolled in a yoga class and also practiced some yoga poses before bed. If she awoke and wasn't back asleep in twenty minutes, she'd get out of bed and practice yoga poses for relaxation. She improved her falling asleep skills and also woke less often during the night.

Kim discovered a simple solution. She focused on relaxing the muscles around her mouth. When she did that, she would fall asleep quickly. This makes sense. Self talk is the source of many sleep problems. You cannot sleep if you are talking to yourself. You will want to stay awake and hear what you are saying! When Kim was relaxing her mouth, tongue, and voice box, she was inhibiting the self-talk bad habit. With her mouth relaxed, she also quieted her mind.

Lynn found that the more he helped his patients learn better sleep habits, the better his own became. So he wrote this book!

The common key here is to keep careful data, in a conscientious sleep diary, and then to systematically experiment. We all sleep, we all, sooner or later, get at least enough sleep to keep ourselves from the daytime hallucinations that people that never sleep will have. The key is to discover what your particular secret for good sleep is. It is like experimenting with a combination lock, where you remember some of the numbers but not the last one, it is vital to try a variety of sleep-enhancing tools to succeed at unlocking the solution to your sleep problems.

GRATITUDE

Finally, you ought to consider the words of the old song.

When I'm worried and I can't sleep
I count my blessings instead of sheep
And I fall asleep counting my blessings
When my bankroll is getting small
I think of when I had none at all
And I fall asleep counting my blessings
    – Irving Berlin, from the movie, *White Christmas*

Research into happiness habits shows clearly that keeping a gratitude diary each day gives you a light in your eyes that spreads joy everywhere. While many insomniacs review their problems and worries as they lie in bed, try reviewing your blessings. Count them, as Irving Berlin suggests, and find your own sleep.

HOMEWORK: How well have you put it all together? Hold yourself accountable and make sure you are making all the changes needed for a foundation of good sleep.

Chapter Ten

Drugs and Sleep

O h, sure, the reader may think, you discourage using drugs to sleep, and now you are going to talk about them? Well, yes, a good point, but the problem is that sometimes there is some use for the drugs. You see, sleep depends on your inner feelings. If you are confident, peaceful, and grateful, and if you have cultivated the capacity to quiet your mind, then you should have no problem learning to sleep better.

But what if you are prone to excess anxiety, and you just cannot quiet the mind? Then certainly drugs may have a place. While they are generally not given for long-term insomnia, it is to your advantage to understand what is available and which of them might work for you.

I must admit, though, that when we look carefully at the outcome research on even the new drugs, they are quite over-rated. They do help sleep, but not by a clinically significant amount. In other words, they may help you, but the behavioral change techniques in this book are the only way to help you teach yourself to have quality sleep. So if you do have to use the drugs, keep experimenting with all the skills we have covered in the book, and eventually wean yourself off the drugs and back to natural sleep.

Over The Counter

Let's start with drugs that don't require a prescription, the over-the-counter drugs (OTCs). The OTCs you get from a pharmacy that are for sleep are basically an antihistamine like

Benedryl™. The antihistamines are helpful if you are trying to dry up an allergy. A side effect is that they do make you sleepy. They also give you quite a dry mouth! Research on these drugs when used to aid sleep is not impressive. They don't work very well.

Some OTC sleep aids will include a pain reliever, such as Tylenol™ or Motrin™. That might be helpful if pain is keeping you awake.

Problems with these OTC medications include developing tolerance for the medication and rebound insomnia. Tolerance means you need more and more of the drug to achieve the same effect. Rebound insomnia means that when you stop taking the drug, you are even more alert and less able to sleep than before you started taking the drug.

Another problem is that by using an OTC drug, you might be masking another problem. Suppose you are actually depressed and when you go to bed, you ruminate and worry. You'd be better off seeing your doctor and looking for the underlying problem so you can treat that.

Herbal Remedies

Melatonin is frequently used for sleep problems. It is a naturally occurring hormone that is produced by the pineal gland, and its purpose seems to be to signal the body that it is time to sleep. It rises when the light goes down. The darker it is, the more melatonin your body will produce.

Some travelers use melatonin to shift their body clock. If you were to go from Los Angeles to New York, you'd be going to bed three hours earlier than your body clock thinks is right. So melatonin might help that situation by convincing the body that it actually is time for bed. Many airline pilots swear by it.

Melatonin is available at pharmacies and health food stores. The doses generally run around one to three milligrams. However, that is actually much more than your body needs or wants. If you are going to use it, a more appropriate dose would be a half or a quarter of a milligram. By the way, this is why many people don't like melatonin. They wake up feeling very drugged and lethargic because they have taken too much of the hormone.

Another problem is that there is a great variation in the purity of melatonin. Because it is not regulated by the Food and Drug Administration, its manufacture is not controlled, so you don't know what you are actually taking.

Now if you are uncomfortable taking a hormone without your doctor's guidance (and I don't blame you for that!), then you might consider that at least two studies found that twenty minutes of meditation before bed will allow the melatonin to naturally rise. Use Autogenic Training before bed.

Valerian Root is a herb that has been used for centuries for nervousness and sleep problems. While it is not as effective as the prescription drugs described in the next section, it seems to be somewhat helpful, according to small clinical trials. It really is a drug, and if you want to use it, you'd be wise to get the advice and guidance of a physician.

Other natural sleep aids include hops, catnip tea, passionflower, and kava. Again, the fact that these are from health food stores doesn't mean they are safe for you. Be careful, and ask your doctor for guidance. Today's physicians have become much more knowledgeable about herbal medicines since so many folks use them.

Prescription Required

Until recently there was no good drug for sleep that did not have a serious potential for habituation (meaning the patient had to take more and more to get the same result) and addiction (that is, when the patient stopped using the drug, there were serious withdrawal symptoms). These drugs were dangerous. Many people did become addicted. Since the withdrawal from an addictive drug is the mirror image of the effects the drug has, the poor patient was caught in a cruel paradox. When the drug was stopped, the insomnia returned with a vengeance! This created some vicious circles, with patients becoming more and more desperate to sleep and M.D.s becoming more and more concerned over addiction.

These problems have been diminished greatly by a new generation of drugs that are far safer and still effective. We will discuss some of them. Bear in mind that new drugs come out from time to time, so when you read this, there may be something newer.

Currently, "consensus guidelines" (rules created by conferences in which experts discuss the evidence and come up with useful rules to follow) recommend using short- or intermediate- acting *benzodiazepine receptor agonist* (BzRA) or *melatonin agonist* drugs. "Agonist" means something that helps or aids a process. If your problem is falling asleep, the guidelines suggest drugs such as benzodiazepine receptor agonist zaleplon (trade names Sonata™ and Starnoc™) and the melatonin- agonist ramelteon (trade name Rozerem™). These are good, because while they help you fall asleep quickly, they leave the body quickly and there is not much danger of you waking up feeling too sedated. Their "half life" (the amount of time it takes half the drug to leave your system) is one to two hours, so they act quickly and leave quickly.

But what if you wake up in the middle of the night or early in the morning? For this pattern, the guidelines suggest that the short-acting drugs are not appropriate, since just as they are going out of your system, you will wake at your problem time. In that case, you will want to try a more intermediate acting drug.

Zolpidem (Ambien™) has a slightly longer half-life of about 2 ½ hours but that is still too short for someone who wakes early in the morning and many people find it not at all helpful. Instead, consider discussing with your doctor the use of either zolpidem controlled release (meaning, the tablet has a quick dissolving layer and then another slow dissolving layer that gives you a new dose of the drug a couple of hours later) or temazepam (Restoril™) which has a half life of around six hours. Temazepam is also much less expensive and if you are not too sedated after eight hours, it may be a help to you.

The drug eszopiclone (Lunesta™) also has a nice long half life and has the advantage, along with zolpidem of being safer for longer term use.

Other drugs that some physicians use include trazodone (Deseryl™) and quetiapine (Seroquel™) but there is not as much research backing up these drugs, so they should generally not be your first choice. Trazodone is an older antidepressant, and quetiapine is a major tranquilizer, so neither was developed with sleep problems in mind. They are generally used when the usual treatments don't seem to do the job.

Some people use drugs like Xanex™ to induce sleep, and that may do that job, but it is not a good drug to use for sleep problems, certainly not one to start with. It doesn't stay in the system long enough and it puts the patient at risk for creating dependency. If you are using this type of drug, talk to your doctor about switching to a better drug, one designed just for sleep.

Generally I would suggest you stay with behavioral approaches to improving sleep. If you gave these a try and you are still suffering, I suggest the prescription drugs rather than the over-the-counter drugs. They work better and the side effects are well known. The newer drugs can be taken for longer times without problems.

But remember, if you take drugs, keep your expectations low. Actual outcomes with drugs are very disappointing. Almost no one on sleep medications actually has the high quality of sleep that you can achieve with the behavioral changes we have discussed. The drugs are over rated, over hyped, and over sold. And while they are safer, they are still not as clean or as safe as changing your own behavior.

Some studies have found that 100% of patients who follow the suggestions in this book improve their sleep to some extent. It is clear that we all can learn to sleep better.

Good luck with your sleep. You should be better at sleep skills if you have worked through the behavior and attitude changes recommended in this book. Every single person has times of good quality sleep. Your challenge is to figure out those times and build on them.

I was always a very light sleeper. It is one of the reasons I have learned so much about sleep.

When I was twelve years old, I had a physical exam from Dr. Conrad McGregor before going to scout camp. "All right," he said, "you're in good enough health. Do you have any complaints?"

"Well, I don't sleep very well."

Dr. Con laughed. "Aw, hell, you wouldn't be Grant and Lorraine's kid if you slept well."

I have learned to sleep much better. You can too.

I genuinely wish you a good night's sleep!

(Look for updates and resources at our website, www.SleepingSkills.com)

ORDER FORM: RELAXATION CD

You may order a CD on relaxation skills (progressive relaxation, autogenic training, mindful breathing skills) for $13.95 including shipping. You may use a check or a credit card. Don't send cash through the mail.

Name:

Address:

City   State   Zip

Credit card no.:

Code number   Expiration Date

(Code is a 3 or 4 digit number, on front of AMEX; back of Visa/MC)

Sign here:

Mail to:

Headacre Press

166 East 5900 South, Ste. B-108

Salt Lake City, UT 84107

You can also purchase and download the audio tracks from our website. www.SleepingSkills.com

NOTES